NEW AMERICANS

Americans from India and Other South Asian Countries

by Ken Park

Series Consultant: Judith A. Warner, Ph.D.,
Professor of Sociology and Criminal Justice,
Texas A&M International University

 **Marshall Cavendish**
Benchmark
New York

Marshall Cavendish Benchmark
99 White Plains Road
Tarrytown, NY 10591
www.marshallcavendish.us

Library of Congress Cataloging-in-Publication Data

Park, Ken.
    Americans from India and other South Asian countries / by Ken Park.
        p. cm. — (New Americans)
    Includes bibliographical references and index.
    ISBN 978-0-7614-4305-6
    1. South Asians--United States—Juvenile literature. 2. East Indians—United States—
    Juvenile literature. 3. South Asian Americans—United States—Juvenile literature.
    4. East Indian Americans—United States—Juvenile literature. 5. Immigrants—United
    States—History—Juvenile literature. 6. South Asia—Emigration and immigration—
    History—Juvenile literature. 7. United States—Emigration and immigration—History—
    Juvenile literature. I. Title.
    E184.S69P366 2010
    304.8'73—dc22   2009002599

Developed for Marshall Cavendish Benchmark by RJF Publishing LLC
Robert Famighetti, President
www.RJFpublishing.com
Design: Westgraphix LLC/Tammy West
Photo Research: Edward A. Thomas
Map Illustrator: Stefan Chabluk
Index: Nila Glikin

Photo credits: Cover, 1, 5, 32, 40, 43, 58, 60, 66, 69: AP/Wide World Photos; 6: © Ambient
Images Inc./Alamy; 10, 36: © Blend Images/Alamy; 18, 55: Getty Images; 19: © Tibor Bognar/
Alamy; 20: Oregon Historical Society. #OrHi 52788; 24: Courtesy of Gloria Saikhon Singh;
25, 54: © Edward A. Thomas; 27: Southern Oregon Historical Society #1603; 28: www.
bhagatsinghthind.com; 31: Harry S. Truman Library; 44: © Frances Roberts/Alamy; 49:
© Charles O. Cecil/Alamy; 53: AFP/Getty Images; 56: iStockphoto; 63: sangament.com/Nisha
Sondhe; 64: © Iain Stuart MacGregor/Alamy; 70: Courtesy of Geeta and Krishen Mehta,
Asia Initiatives.

Cover: Devotees attend the opening of a new Hindu temple in Georgia.

Printed in Malaysia.

135642

Publisher's Note: A number of people, including recent immigrants from South Asia or their
descendants, were interviewed for this book. When interviewees so requested, real names
were changed. All cases where name changes were made are indicated within the text of
the book.

CONTENTS

Words defined in the glossary are in **bold** type
the first time they appear in the text.

INTRODUCTION

The United States has embraced immigration for most of its history—and has been a destination of choice for people seeking a better life. Today hundreds of thousands of immigrants arrive each year to live and work and make their way in a new country. These "New Americans" come for many reasons, and they come from places all over the world. They bring with them new customs, languages, and traditions—and face many challenges in their adopted country. Over time, they and their children are changed by and become part of the American mainstream culture. At the same time, the mainstream is itself changed as it absorbs many elements of the immigrants' cultures, from ethnic foods to ideas from non-Western belief systems. An understanding of the New Americans, and how they will form part of the American future, is essential for everyone.

This series focuses on recent immigrants from eight major countries and regions: the Caribbean and Central America, China, India and other South Asian countries, Korea, Mexico, Russia and Eastern Europe, Southeast Asia, and West Africa.

Each of these geographic areas is a major source of the millions of immigrants who have come to the United States in the last decades of the twentieth century and the beginning of the twenty-first. For many of these people, the opportunity to move to the United States was opened up by the major

New Americans being sworn in as U.S. citizens.

changes in U.S. immigration law that occurred in the 1960s. For others, the opportunity or imperative to immigrate was triggered by events in their own countries, such as the collapse of Communism in Eastern Europe or civil wars in Central America.

Some of the New Americans found sizable communities of Americans from the same ethnic background and had the benefit of "ethnic neighborhoods" to move into where they could feel welcome and get help adjusting to American life. Many of these communities originated in a previous major wave of immigration, from the 1880s to 1920. Some of the New Americans found very few predecessors to ease the transition as they faced the challenges of adjustment.

These volumes tell the stories of the New Americans, including the personal accounts of a number of immigrants and their children who agreed to be interviewed by some of the authors. As you read, you will learn about the countries of origin and the cultures of these newcomers to American society. You will learn, as well, about how the New Americans are enriching, as they adapt to, American life.

Judith A. Warner, Ph.D.
Professor of Sociology and Criminal Justice
Texas A&M International University

Shops in this Indian-American neighborhood in New York City feature clothing and other products and services that cater to local residents.

CHAPTER ONE

THE SOUTH ASIAN-AMERICAN COMMUNITY TODAY

South Asia is a densely populated region on the other side of the world from the United States. About 1.5 billion people live in the six South Asian countries of India, Pakistan, Bangladesh, Sri Lanka, Nepal, and Bhutan.

Since the year 2000, almost 100,000 South Asians have made the long journey to immigrate to the United States each year. That makes South Asians one of the fastest growing immigrant groups in the United States.

In 2006, according to U.S. Census Bureau estimates, almost 3 million people of South Asian heritage lived in the United States. That number represented about one percent of all U.S. residents. It included foreign-born immigrants and people born in the United States of South Asian descent. As the number of South Asian Americans grows, so do their contributions to American society and its future—in medicine, technology, government, entertainment, and many other fields.

For example, when the U.S. national junior cricket team takes the field, most of the eleven boys playing for the United States are descendants of South Asian immigrants. (Cricket is a popular game in many parts of the world and has many similarities with baseball.) When you're on YouTube or Facebook, you're probably using technologies developed by South Asian Americans. And, of course, anyone who likes spicy curried chicken or chewy *roti* bread is enjoying foods brought to the Americas from South Asia.

This book tells the history of South Asian immigrants who have come to the United States. It describes some of what it's like to be *Desi*. *Desi* is a word in the ancient **Sanskrit** language of India that means "one from our country." Today, it's a word South Asian Americans use to describe themselves.

South Asian Americans reflect the diversity of their homelands. Many come to the United States speaking English. But South Asians may also speak Hindi, Bengali, Gujarati, Marathi, Tamil, Telugu, Urdu, Punjabi, or one of another dozen or so South Asian languages. The religion of most South Asians is **Hinduism**, but many South Asians practice **Islam** (these people are called **Muslims**) or **Sikhism**. They come from big cities and from small Indian towns.

Many South Asian Americans are professionals and managers: doctors, engineers, and business executives. Overall, South Asians have been as successful as just about

States with the Most Indian Americans

California	475,118
New York	349,290
New Jersey	256,965
Texas	194,908
Illinois	166,870
Florida	117,195
Pennsylvania	84,111
Virginia	76,167
Georgia	74,525
Michigan	71,757

Source: U.S. Bureau of the Census, 2006 estimates

any immigrant group in the United States. But many newer South Asian immigrants live in poverty, seeking work or toiling long hours in an effort to find their share of the American dream.

By the Numbers

The U.S. Census Bureau's American Community Survey estimated that in 2006 there were 2,482,141 people of Indian heritage and 194,462 people of Pakistani heritage living in the United States. About three-quarters of those people were born outside the United States.

The Indian-American community includes many doctors and other highly skilled professionals.

In 2000, the U.S. Census Bureau counted 95,295 people in the United States who had been born in Bangladesh, 25,265 who had been born in Sri Lanka, and 11,715 who had been born in Nepal. The number of Bhutanese living in the United States was probably less than 1,000, according to the 2000 Census.

When immigrants first come to the United States, they are likely to move to urban areas. Big cities such as New York, Chicago, and Los Angeles provide job opportunities. Immigrants also tend to settle in communities in cities where other people from their country already live. Such cities are called **gateway cities**.

South Asian Americans live primarily in the largest cities and states. More South Asian Americans live in California than in any other state, followed by New York, New Jersey, Texas, Illinois, and Florida. The thirteen communities with the highest percentage of Pakistani immigrants in 2000 were all in New Jersey, Texas, Virginia, California, or Illinois.

While there are many prominent South Asian communities in the United States, gateway cities have been somewhat less important for South Asians than for some other immigrant groups. The first South Asian immigrants came by ship to California in the early 1900s. But those immigrants faced a political climate hostile to Asian immigration. By the late 1960s, when immigration from South Asia began to increase again, those original immigrant communities were both sparse and small.

Beginning in the late 1960s, South Asians were able to immigrate directly to where the jobs were—major cities that offered medical, scientific, and technical jobs. For South Asians, this meant settling not only in traditional gateway metropolitan areas like Chicago and New York but also, more recently, in "emerging" gateway cities such as Dallas–Fort Worth, Atlanta, and Washington, D.C. (Immigrating to an East Coast city such as Washington, D.C., does not involve a longer journey than going to a city in California. India is actually closer to the East Coast of the United States than it is to the West Coast.)

Economic Success

Census data show that many South Asians have been successful in the United States. There are many reasons for this success. Many South Asians, both men and women, come to the United States as well-educated professionals. Many arrive already speaking English. Also, South Asian immigrants include a relatively high percentage of women. A mix of men and women helps to lend stability to immigrant communities and daily life.

Education, strong family structure, and English-language skills are considered "human capital"—essentially, they are strengths that people have acquired or cultural values they live by that contribute to success. The general success of South Asian Americans is attributable in large measure to their extensive human capital.

Many South Asians initially come to the United States as **temporary residents** to fill a job or to study, rather than as immigrants with **permanent resident status**. But many Indian students and temporary workers go on to establish

South Asian Americans and the U.S. U15 Cricket Team

Cricket is a game that dates back at least to the sixteenth century. It became very popular in Great Britain, and its popularity spread to areas that became British colonies (including the present-day South Asian countries of India, Pakistan, Bangladesh, and Sri Lanka). Matches are played between two teams of eleven players each. The game has some resemblance to baseball; a member of one team throws a ball to a member of the opposing team, who uses a special bat to hit the ball and attempts to score runs.

In the summer of 2008, the U.S. national cricket team for players under fifteen years old won second place in the Americas Champions tournament. Most of the players were South Asian Americans. Team captain Abhijit Joshi was named the best batter of the tournament, which was held in Bermuda. Joshi scored sixty-eight runs when the United States beat Bermuda to earn second place. He hit three "sixes," the cricket version of home runs.

Boys on the team came from Texas, Illinois, New York, and other states. Almost all the players were born in the United States. But their families came from areas where cricket is very popular, including India and Pakistan.

The national cricket teams of India and Pakistan are fierce rivals. But on the U15 USA National Team, boys of Indian, Pakistani, and West Indian descent all get along, says coach Anwer Khan, who played cricket around the world: "We are all together. There is no difference. We try to do the best for the USA."

permanent residence in the United States and eventually become U.S. citizens, according to a U.S. government report. In 2007, more than 88,000 Indian students and their families (spouses and children) received **visas** to study in the United States. More than 300,000 workers and their families from India had **temporary work visas**. Many of these people (after graduation or after working for a time) are sponsored by an employer or prospective employer to obtain permanent resident status.

The incomes of Indian Americans are often higher than the incomes of most Americans. In 2006, 50 percent of Indian-American families earned $87,484 or more, and 50 percent earned less (this middle point that divides a group exactly in half is called the median). That's almost $30,000 above the median family income of $58,526 for the total U.S. population. Only 8 percent of Indian Americans lived in poverty (as defined by the U.S. government) in 2006, according to the Census Bureau. The national poverty rate at that time was 13 percent. The situation was not as good for Pakistani Americans. Their median family income was about the same as the figure for all Americans, and about 17 percent of Pakistani Americans lived in poverty.

Indian and Pakistani Americans are twice as likely as the average American to have a college degree. In 2006, more than two-thirds—69 percent—of Indian-American adults and more than half—54 percent—of Pakistani-American adults had college degrees. Among the general population, only 27 percent of adults had college degrees. This high level of education helped South Asian Americans to get good jobs. Almost two-thirds (65 percent) of Indian Americans worked in management, professional, or similar fields in 2006, whereas only 37 percent of all U.S. workers did so. Pakistani Americans were also slightly more likely than Americans as a whole to be professionals or managers.

Many Indian and Pakistani Americans own small businesses. The name Patel, which suggests that the person is an immigrant from Gujarat, India, is common among those who own small hotels. The more than 9,000 members of the Asian American Hotel Owners Association own more than 22,000 hotels. In 2008, the association was led by Chairman Ashwin "Ash" Patel, Vice Chairman Tarun Patel, Secretary Chandra I. Patel, and Treasurer Hemant D. Patel. South Asians are also prominent among the owners of Dunkin' Donuts, Subway, and other convenience-store franchises.

Family and family life are very important to South Asians and South Asian Americans. Indian, Pakistani, and Bangladeshi Americans more than fifteen years of age are much more likely to be married than are people over fifteen in the overall U.S. population. Nearly 70 percent of Indian Americans, 69 percent of Bangladeshi Americans, and 62 percent of Pakistani Americans over fifteen were married in 2006, compared to only about 50 percent of the overall U.S. population.

Citizenship

When immigrants come to a new country, many dream of returning home some day. South Asians who can afford it often travel back to their homelands to visit. But once in the United States as permanent residents, many South Asians become American citizens. About 55 percent of foreign-born Pakistani Americans and 45 percent of foreign-born Indian Americans have completed the **naturalization** process and become citizens. In contrast, 42 percent of all foreign-born residents have become citizens.

As with all immigrant groups, some South Asians come to or stay in the United States without obtaining the required U.S. government documents. These people are described as undocumented aliens. About half the South Asian undocumented aliens are people who enter the United States with legal temporary student or tourist visas but then stay on after those visas expire.

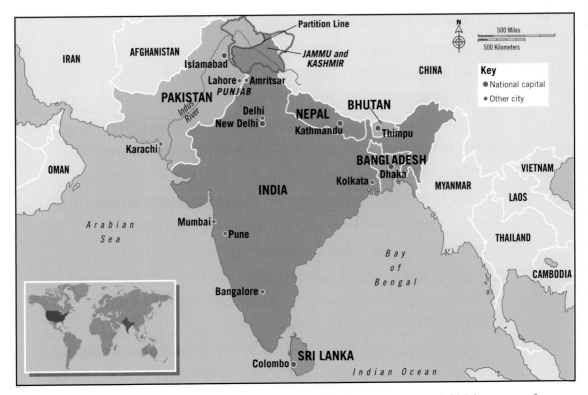

The six-country region of South Asia is home to 1.5 billion people. India is the region's largest country, in both size and population.

According to the U.S. Department of Homeland Security, there were about 11.5 million "unauthorized," or undocumented, immigrants in the United States in January 2006. About 270,000, or 2 percent, of the total were from India.

South Asia: Ancient and Modern

More than one-fifth of the world's people live in South Asia. By far the largest and most populous country in the region is India. Pakistan and Bangladesh are also very populous nations. Sri Lanka is an island nation southeast of India. Nepal and Bhutan are mountainous countries located between India and China.

The civilization of the Indian subcontinent (as South Asia is sometimes called) is one of the oldest in the world. By 2500 B.C.E., people in the Indus River valley (in what is now India and Pakistan) were building cities of brick.

Over the centuries, many peoples ruled over different parts of India, which historically included present-day Pakistan and Bangladesh. The seeds of the Hindu religion, which is dominant today in India, were planted with the arrival of Aryan peoples around 1700 B.C.E. Arab invaders in the eighth century C.E. introduced Islam to India. About 97 percent of Pakistanis and 83 percent of Bangladeshis today are Muslims, or followers of Islam.

From the 1500s into the 1800s, India was ruled by Mughal emperors. By the mid–1700s, different Mughal rulers had weak control over different parts of India, and Great Britain, through the British East India Company, was exerting ever more control over the region. On November 1, 1858, Britain asserted its direct government control over the "princes, chiefs and people of India."

From the late nineteenth century, Indians, led by the Indian National Congress and later also the Muslim League, increasingly opposed British rule. Indian leader Mohandas Gandhi led massive nonviolent campaigns against British rule beginning in the 1930s. After World War II (1939–1945), Britain agreed to grant India independence. In the period 1945–1947, Indian leaders who negotiated with the British sought independence plans that would satisfy both the Hindu majority and the Muslim minority, which feared Hindu rule. In 1947, when India became independent from Britain, the Islamic-majority areas became the separate country of Pakistan. Pakistan originally had two parts. Bangladesh, formerly East Pakistan, became a separate country in 1971 after a war in which Pakistan surrendered its former territory. Sri Lanka (then Ceylon) gained its independence from Britain in 1948.

Today, India is the world's largest democracy. The nation's more than one billion people represent a diverse mix of cultures. Since major economic reforms in the 1990s, the Indian economy has been among the fastest growing in the world. Despite economic growth that gives India the world's largest middle class (some 300 million people), 267 million people in the country were living on

Mohandas Gandhi (*right*) leads a 1930 march protesting British rule.

Mumbai is
India's largest city and an
important business and financial center.

the equivalent of less than one dollar a day in 2005, according to the World Bank.

Pakistan also has a democratic government, although there have been periods when the military has overthrown an elected leader. Because there are bases for terrorists widely believed to be in Pakistan's North-West Frontier Province and other areas, immigrants to the United States from Pakistan can be subjected to unusually strict scrutiny. Pakistan and India remain rival nations.

In 2006, the United States and Nepal agreed to a plan to help ethnic Nepalese who had been living in refugee camps since the late 1980s. Some have resettled in the United States, including in Minnesota, where the Minneapolis area has a thriving Nepalese-American community.

This 1909 photograph shows Punjabi-immigrant railroad workers in Oregon.

CHAPTER TWO

EARLIER GENERATIONS

Today, people fly from India to the United States in less than twenty-four hours. People in the United States can reach people in South Asia instantly by telephone. But in the 1800s, traveling the 7,500 miles (12,000 kilometers) from India to the U.S. West Coast took weeks by ship. There was no international phone calling. With such a separation between South Asia and the United States, it is not surprising that immigration records show that fewer than one thousand Indians came to the United States during the 1800s.

From the Punjab to California
But beginning around 1900, thousands of people (almost all of them men) immigrated from the **Punjab** region in northwest India to British Columbia in Canada and to

California. Information about the United States had reached some Punjabis through British soldiers stationed in India. A number of Punjabi immigrants had been soldiers and policemen themselves and had heard about the United States during their service.

The immigrants heard that they could earn much better wages in the United States than they could in the Punjab. So they took a chance and traveled to the United States. To pay for the trip, immigrants often borrowed money. Sometimes families mortgaged, or took out loans on, their land to support a young man's journey. Many immigrants hoped to return home after earning and saving money in the United States.

Journeys could begin with a train trip east across India to the port of Kolkata (formerly called Calcutta). Then immigrants would take a steamship to the port of Hong Kong, on the coast of China. The voyage across the Pacific Ocean from Hong Kong to California took about eighteen days. The *San Francisco Chronicle* newspaper on April 6, 1899, described several of the Punjabi newcomers:

> "The four Sikhs who arrived on the *Nippon Maru* the other day were permitted yesterday to land by the immigration officials. The quartet formed the most picturesque group that has been seen on the Pacific Mall dock for many a day. One of them, Bakkshlled [sic] Singh, speaks English with fluency, the others just a little. . . . All of them have been soldiers and policemen."

Most of the first Punjabi immigrants were followers of the Sikh religion. Sikh men wear distinctive turbans to cover their hair, which their religion forbids them to cut. Even though most immigrants were Sikhs, Americans usually referred to all early South Asian immigrants as Hindus or "Hindoos."

Working on the West Coast

In the early 1900s, some two thousand Indians worked on crews that built railroads, most of them working on the Southern Pacific Railroad, which ran from California east through Arizona and New Mexico and on into Texas. Other Punjabis worked in lumber mills or fish canneries in northern California and the Pacific Northwest. Many worked on farms. Early Indian immigration reached a peak in the period 1907–1910. The total number of South Asians in the United States at that time was about seven thousand. Almost all of them lived in the West Coast states of California, Oregon, and Washington.

Parts of California, like the Sacramento Valley in central California, reminded the Punjabis of home. Like the Punjab in India, the Sacramento Valley was a fertile farming region. Thanks to irrigation, California was becoming a major agricultural area. Farm workers, most of whom did not speak much English, often traveled and worked as a group. A "boss man" or "gang boss" who spoke English would arrange their jobs. The immigrants did jobs like cutting asparagus spears. "Walk and bend, bend and walk" for ten to fourteen hours a day was how one Sikh laborer described the hard work. Using their experience from India, Punjabis also played a role in California's early rice farms.

Punjabi-Mexican Families

Families with a Punjabi husband and a Mexican-American wife were most common in the Imperial Valley, in southern California. Punjabi immigrants and Mexican Americans had much in common. They were looked down upon and treated as outsiders by many Americans. They shared the rural life. The roti bread of India was similar to the tortillas of Mexico. Two of the first couples to get married were Valentina Alvarez and Rullia Singh and Rosario Perez and Purn Singh. It was common for several women in the same Mexican-American family to marry Punjabis.

Rosario Perez and Purn Singh on their wedding day.

When the immigrants were able to save money, they often pooled their funds to buy or lease land. By 1920, Punjabi immigrants owned or leased nearly 90,000 acres (36,425 hectares) of farmland in California.

Sikh immigrants usually chose to live among other Sikhs, often in camps or boarding houses. Many of the men were married to women who had stayed behind in India. Those men who were single when they arrived often did not marry because there were few Punjabi women in the United States for them to wed. Many states during this period had what were called anti-miscegenation laws (laws that prohibited people of different races from marrying each other). These laws were aimed at keeping dark-skinned people, including South Asian immigrants, from marrying white women. Some Punjabi men who stayed in the United States married women of Mexican descent, which was not prohibited by the anti-miscegenation laws.

Sikhs built temples, or *gurdwaras*, in several California cities, including Stockton and Yuba City. Gurdwaras served as both community centers and places of worship.

Sikh immigrants began building gurdwaras on the West Coast in the early 1900s. Today, gurdwaras, such as this one in New Jersey, can be found in many parts of the United States.

Facing Prejudice and Barriers to Immigration

The Punjabis came to the United States at a time when prejudice against other Asians was already widespread. Many Americans viewed Chinese, Japanese, and Indian workers as competitors for jobs. Some U.S. workers had recently formed labor unions and had succeeded in winning higher pay for themselves. They feared that the competition from immigrants would lower their pay because employers could get the immigrants to work for less money than the native-born, unionized Americans. Therefore, they reasoned, native-born Americans would not get jobs unless they too accepted the lower pay scale. Some Americans were also suspicious of Asian immigrants' different cultures.

The Asiatic Exclusion League (AEL), backed by labor unions, was founded in San Francisco in 1905. It was dedicated to "the preservation of the Caucasian race [white people] upon the American soil." The AEL was founded to oppose Japanese immigration, but it also came to oppose South Asian immigration. Eventually, pressure from groups like the AEL led to laws that restricted immigration and immigrants' rights.

In 1913, California passed the Alien Land Law. This law essentially made it illegal for Asian immigrants to buy land in the state. The law was aimed primarily at Japanese immigrants but also applied to Indians. California passed other laws in 1920 and 1921 that imposed further restrictions on what immigrants could own. In order to get around the Alien Land Law, some Punjabi immigrants entered business partnerships with whites; land was owned in the name of the white partner. In families with a Punjabi husband and Mexican-American wife, the wife could own land in her name, since Mexican Americans' right to own land was not restricted by the law. The 1913 law was eventually overturned by the U.S. Supreme Court, but not until 1952. The 1920 and 1921 laws were eventually repealed by the voters of California in 1956.

In 1917, the federal Immigration Act passed by Congress included provisions that barred immigration to the United States from almost all countries in South and East Asia. That meant that Indian immigrants

"Hindus" Run Out of Town

Immigrants from India faced racism of many kinds in the United States. Sometimes opposition to immigrants became violent.

In August 1907, union leaders in Bellingham, in the state of Washington, warned the owners of lumber mills in the area that they did not want Indian immigrants to be working in the mills after Labor Day, September 2. But the Indian immigrants continued to work. On the night of Wednesday, September 4, a crowd estimated at about five hundred workers attacked the area near the waterfront where the immigrant workers lived. The mob beat immigrants and destroyed buildings. The police took the Indian immigrants to the City Hall to escape the violence.

The mayor vowed to protect the immigrants' rights. The local newspaper condemned the riots. But it also said, "The Hindu is not a good citizen. . . . Our cloak of brotherly love is not large enough to include him as a member" of the community. By Saturday, September 7, the several hundred Indian immigrant workers in Bellingham had all left town.

A group of Punjabi immigrants in Washington around 1900. Some white Americans considered the immigrants unwelcome competition for jobs.

Bhagat Singh Thind, whose citizenship case reached the U.S. Supreme Court, is shown here in uniform while serving in the U.S. Army during World War I.

already in the United States would not even be able to bring their families or relatives to the country to join them.

The Immigration Act of 1924 set limits on new immigration from countries around the world and established immigration quotas that were based on the number of people from a country who were already living in the United States in 1890. Under this law, which strongly favored immigrants from Northern and Western Europe, the quota for India was set at one hundred immigrants per year.

Deciding Who Could Be a "White" Citizen

The 1917 Immigration Act raised the question of whether people already in the United States who came from what were called barred countries could become U.S. citizens.

That question reached the U.S. Supreme Court in a 1923 case called *U.S.* v. *Bhagat Singh Thind*. Bhagat Singh Thind was an immigrant from the city of Amritsar in the Punjab. He came to the United States in 1913 and worked in lumber mills in Oregon. He attended the University of California and served in the U.S. Army in World War I. (The United States fought in World War I in 1917–1918.) In 1920, he was approved to become a naturalized citizen, but that decision was challenged by a naturalization examiner.

When Thind's case reached the U.S. Supreme Court, the issue was whether Thind fit the legal definition of a "free white person." If he did, he would be eligible to become a naturalized citizen under a federal law passed in 1795. Thind argued that he was a member of the Caucasian race and therefore should be considered "white" under the law. The Supreme Court ruled that though Thind might be a Caucasian, he was not a "white person" as was generally understood in "common speech." He therefore could not become a citizen. In the court's ruling, Justice George Sutherland wrote, "The

Fighting for India in the United States

In part because of the **discrimination** they faced in Canada and the United States, some South Asian immigrants joined the Gadar (also sometimes spelled Ghadar) Party, which advocated the overthrow of British rule in India. They published the first Gadar newspaper in San Francisco in 1913. One leader was Lala Har Dayal, a lecturer in Indian philosophy at Stanford University, in California. He was arrested in the United States at the request of the British but left for Switzerland while out on bail.

The Gadar Party's efforts to inspire a revolt in India during World War I (1914–1918) were unsuccessful. Some members of the party in the United States were convicted in San Francisco in 1918 of plotting against India. While awaiting the verdict in the courtroom, one defendant, Ram Singh, shot and killed a co-defendant, Ram Chandra, who was believed to have used the group's funds for his own purposes.

The First Indian-American Congressman

In 1956, Dalip Singh Saund (1899–1973) became the first Asian American elected to the U.S. House of Representatives. He was elected to represent Riverside and Imperial counties in California.

Born in the Punjab in 1899, Saund came to the United States in 1920. He earned a doctorate at the University of California. He later became a lettuce farmer in southern California's Imperial Valley and helped organize the Indian Association of America to fight for passage of the 1946 Luce-Celler Act, which eased immigration restrictions and allowed immigrants from India to become U.S. citizens. He became a citizen after the bill became law.

Saund was a Democrat and a Sikh. His election campaign against Jacqueline Cochran Odlum, a famous aviator, in 1956, drew national attention. In Congress, he supported farm subsidies and urged that the United States give aid directly to towns and regions in foreign countries, rather than to the central government of those countries, which he believed would lead to corruption. Saund was re-elected in 1958 and 1960. He suffered a stroke while campaigning in 1962 and was not re-elected.

physical group characteristics of the Hindus render them readily distinguishable" from Americans "commonly recognized as white." Despite losing his case, Thind remained in the United States. He was an author and religious teacher until his death, in 1967. The legal **precedent** set by his case was reversed by federal legislation in 1946.

With immigration virtually barred and citizenship discouraged, the number of South Asians in the United States declined from the 1920s through the mid-1940s. Many Indians returned home, which had been the plan of some when they arrived. There were fewer than 2,500 in the United States in 1940.

The Door to the United States Reopens a Crack

In 1941, the United States entered World War II against Germany and Japan and their allies. Americans generally

President Harry S.
Truman signs the 1946 law easing
immigration restrictions against people from India and
allowing Indian immigrants to become citizens.

favored helping the Asian nations (including India, then still a British colony) that were fighting with the United States and its allies against Japan. In 1943, immigration and naturalization restrictions against people from China were eased. Indians and Filipinos won similar status in 1946 with the passage of legislation authored by Representatives Clare Booth Luce and Emanuel Celler. The law eased immigration restrictions against people from India and allowed Indian immigrants in the United States to become naturalized citizens. In the 1950s, 1,850 Indians immigrated to the United States, according to U.S. immigration data. But the South Asian population was still below 30,000 in 1960.

At Liberty Island in New York Harbor, President Lyndon Johnson
signs the 1965 law that dramatically changed immigration policy
and paved the way for a new wave of South Asian immigrants.
Liberty Island is the home of the Statue of Liberty, which
at the beginning of the century had welcomed millions of
immigrants arriving from Europe.

CHAPTER THREE

THE NEW IMMIGRANTS

For much of the twentieth century, U.S. immigration law severely limited immigration from Asia. From 1920 through 1959, Asians made up fewer than one percent of all immigrants entering the United States. This situation changed dramatically after the passage of the Immigration and Nationality Act of 1965. This law, by largely ending quotas based on national origin, significantly increased opportunities for immigration from South Asia.

The act changed the rules for admitting immigrants to the United States by focusing on two goals: supporting the reunification of family members and encouraging immigration by people with certain highly desired occupational skills. The new law allowed for an annual total of 170,000

Starting an Immigration Web

In 1969, Dr. Amin (name changed to protect privacy) from a village in Gujarat, India, was working in Great Britain. He saw an ad in a medical journal offering free room and board (housing and meals) to doctors who wanted to work at an urban hospital in New Jersey. Dr. Amin and his wife decided to move to New Jersey. Their young daughter, who had been staying in India with grandparents, joined them. The Amins thought Dr. Amin would get more training and experience in New Jersey, then return to India.

But, as Dr. Amin rose to become a prominent surgeon at the hospital, he decided to become a U.S. citizen. He eventually sponsored several dozen of his relatives who wanted to immigrate to the United States. This kind of pattern in which one immigrant sponsors others, who may in turn sponsor still others, is called an immigration web. Forty years after arriving in the United States, Dr. Amin, who still thinks about returning to India, has five American-born grandchildren.

immigrants from the Eastern Hemisphere (which includes Europe, Africa, and Asia) and 120,000 from the Western Hemisphere (North and South America). The limit on immigrants from any one country in the Eastern Hemisphere was 20,000. The law also reserved 10 percent of immigration visas for "qualified immigrants who were members of the professions." Those visas were awarded on a first-come, first-served basis. Whereas immigration laws since the 1920s strongly favored immigrants from Northern and Western Europe, people from countries in this region no longer had preference under the new act.

The 1965 law also reserved about 55 percent of visas for people who were family members of citizens and 20 percent for spouses and unmarried children of "permanent residents"—immigrants who had not become citizens. But, even more important in the long run, the new law ended any numerical limits on immigration by immediate family members—parents, spouses, and children—of U.S.

citizens. These provisions aimed at making family reunification easier created many opportunities for immigrants who had come to the United States to sponsor extended family to join them. In turn, those family members could sponsor further extended family to join them. This phenomenon is sometimes referred to as chain migration or an immigration web.

Doctors and Other Professionals Immigrate

In 1965, the United States also passed new laws that established the Medicare and Medicaid public health programs. They provided federal funding to help older people and the poor afford medical care. The new laws meant that more people could get health care. But U.S. medical schools were not training enough physicians to meet the new demand. That situation, combined with the immigration law changes, created opportunities for doctors from South Asia (and other regions of the world). From 1965 through 1974, 75,000 foreign doctors came to the United States. This meant that by 1974, about 20 percent of doctors in the United States were foreign born.

South Asian scientists and engineers also immigrated in the late 1960s and early 1970s to work in the growing defense and space industries. Many South Asian students were also coming to the United States to study at American colleges and universities under **nonimmigrant visas**. Many of these students were able to establish permanent resident status as immigrants once they were offered jobs in the United States after graduation.

A number of South Asian immigrants first enter the United States on student visas allowing them to study at American universities.

The immigration of students and professionals and of the family members who were able to come to the United States because of the emphasis on family reunification explains how the number of immigrants from South Asia soared in the years after 1965. Indian immigration grew to about 15,000 people a year in the 1970s and to more than 79,000 in 2005. The number of Indians who immigrated in 2005 alone would be enough to create a city the size of Canton, Ohio, or Lawrence, Kansas.

Why South Asians Came to the United States

What was happening in the United States was only half the immigration story. India, Pakistan, and Sri Lanka (then called Ceylon) had become independent from Great Britain

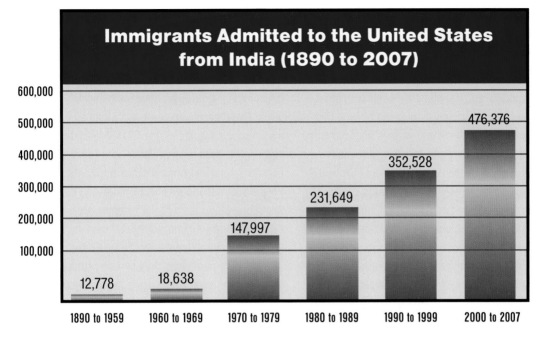

Immigrants Admitted to the United States from India (1890 to 2007)

Source: U.S. Department of Homeland Security, Office of Immigration Statistics, *2007 Yearbook of Immigration Statistics*

in 1947 and 1948. At that time, there was very little industry in those nations. The British colonial economic system was set up to direct raw materials, such as Indian cotton, back to British industries for processing.

Once the countries they led had won their independence, South Asian leaders took steps to build up their economies. India's first prime minister, Jawaharlal Nehru, built on the existing British education system. He helped develop schools for science and engineering to move the country forward. The government also sponsored students who wanted to study overseas.

In addition, Nehru established a "planned economy" for India. This meant that the government, rather than individual people or businesses, planned much of what happened

The Immigration Process and Documents

Foreign citizens who want to immigrate to the United States need to get U.S. government approval and documents. (People who enter the United States without going through this process are often referred to as undocumented immigrants; they can be returned to their homeland by the U.S. government.) Since U.S. law favors immigrants who are joining family members or coming to fill a job, most immigrants who come to the United States are in one of these preference categories.

Such immigrants start the approval process with an immigrant visa petition. The petition is submitted by a person's "sponsor" in the United States, either a family member or potential employer. The petition gives information about the immigrant and the sponsor. It is submitted to U.S. Citizenship and Immigration Services, a division of the Department of Homeland Security.

If the petition is approved, the potential immigrant then goes on a waiting list to get an immigrant visa number, issued by the U.S. Department of State. The total number of immigrants allowed to enter the United States each year is limited by U.S. law. So it may take several years for a person to get an immigrant visa number. Once a petitioner gets that number, the person can go to a U.S. consulate in his or her country to get an immigrant visa. The immigrant visa allows the person to move permanently to the United States.

People without family or employer sponsors can enter the United States in several other ways. If they are fleeing persecution in their home country, they can be granted refugee or asylum status to live in the United States. A different path is to enter the annual Diversity Visa Lottery program for immigrant visas. The chances are small: more than 9 million people applied for the 50,000 available visas in the 2009 lottery. Visa recipients are chosen at random from among all applicants. People from nations with high immigration to the United States already—for example, Mexico, China, and India—are not eligible for the lottery.

People can also enter the United States with nonimmigrant visas. Tourist visas, student visas, and temporary work visas, for example, allow people to come to the United States for a limited period of time. If during that time a visa holder can find an employer sponsor, he or she can then apply for a permanent resident visa.

A permanent resident can become a naturalized citizen usually after living in the United States for five years. To become a naturalized citizen, a person must be at least eighteen years old and "of good moral character." Applicants go through a naturalization interview to determine whether they are in any way undesirable applicants. An applicant must also take a naturalization exam. The exam tests for a basic understanding of English, U.S. history, and U.S. government. If approved, immigrants usually attend a naturalization ceremony. They swear allegiance to the United States and officially become citizens.

The Fourteenth Amendment to the U.S. Constitution guarantees citizenship at birth to almost all individuals born in the United States. This is so even if their parents are undocumented immigrants.

in the economy. The government limited the amount of investments that could be made by foreigners, so that foreigners could not exert the same control over India that the British had. Economic gains would directly benefit the Indian people, most of whom were extremely poor.

But the planned economy also had the effect of discouraging individual innovation and **entrepreneurs**. Restrictions made it difficult to start new businesses. That meant that many of the engineers, scientists, and businesspeople being trained in India could not find what they considered suitable job opportunities there. In the 1960s, a growing amount of information was available in South Asia about the United States. Relatives who traveled abroad by plane brought home stories about American life. Also, advances in communications—such as television—gave South Asians a greater understanding of the United States. When the U.S. government changed its immigration policy in the late 1960s, adventurous South Asians got the opportunity to pursue their careers—and much higher salaries—in the United States.

A New Type of Immigrant, Mostly

The South Asians who came to the United States after 1965 tended to be different from the Punjabi immigrants who had come at the start of the century. The new immigrants were mostly well-educated, professional people. Most came from well-to-do and middle-class families in India. Most spoke English because that language had been the language of India during the years of British rule.

The South Asian new immigrants were also different from the earlier immigrants in another way. They were a diverse group whose members came from various regions of the subcontinent. They spoke a variety of languages besides English, followed different religions, and had different cultures. From India, major groups included Gujarati speakers from the Gujarat region in northwestern India and Hindi speakers from northern and central India. Most of the Indian immigrants were Hindu, but the Hindu religion has many regional variations. There were also Sikhs from the Indian Punjab. Most immigrants from Pakistan and some Indian immigrants spoke Urdu. Bangladeshi immi-

Many South Asian immigrants have found work in the high-tech industries in California's Silicon Valley.

South Asian Immigration in 2006

Country	Country Population	Percentage of South Asian Population	Immigrants to the United States in 2006	Percentage of 2006 South Asian Immigrants
India	1,129,866,164	75%	61,369	62%
Pakistan	164,741,924	11%	17,418	18%
Bangladesh	150,448,339	10%	14,644	15%
Nepal	28,901,790	2%	3,733	4%
Sri Lanka	20,926,315	1%	2,192	2%
Bhutan	2,327,849	0%	78	0%
TOTAL	1,497,212,381	100%	99,434	100%

Sources: "Persons Obtaining Legal Permanent Resident Status by Region and Country of Origin, Fiscal Years 1997 to 2006," Department of Homeland Security; U.S. Census Bureau, Population Division/International Programs Center.

Note: The percentage columns do not add to 100 because of rounding.

grants, most of whom spoke Bengali, were, like Pakistanis, predominantly Muslim.

The new immigrants settled throughout the United States. While California was a popular destination, so were other states with large cities. The new immigrants found work in large hospitals in big cities like Chicago and New York and in the defense and space industries of Texas, Florida, and the West Coast. When the information technology industry boomed in the 1990s, Silicon Valley in California (south of San Francisco) became a major destination.

But the new immigrants also had some things in common with the first South Asian immigrants. They came

One Family's Story: From India to New Jersey

The paths taken by Vikram and Rekha Ganvir (names changed at their request) from India to Jersey City, New Jersey, illustrate a path taken by many Desis. Vikram came to Hawaii in 1991 from Lucknow, India, on a student visa to study for his doctorate in history. He moved to California during the Internet boom and later moved to New York. Vikram was joined by his wife, Rekha, from New Delhi after their marriage, in India, in 2003. Vikram worked at a company operating a Web portal for Indian **expatriates**, and Rekha worked at a nonprofit organization that gives funding to nongovernmental organizations (NGOs) providing services in India. Soon they both established permanent residency. Like most Indian immigrants, Rekha and Vikram came to the United States "to study and explore work opportunities," Rekha said. "We weren't escaping anything. There is a lot of exciting stuff going on in India, and we hope to return one day."

to the United States with the support of their families. They came to pursue a better life. And many thought they would probably return to South Asia at some point.

The Tech Boom

Besides those arriving with permanent resident visas, South Asians continued to come to the United States in large numbers as students and as temporary workers. The technology industry boom that started in the 1990s helped Indians become the largest group receiving temporary work visas. In 2005, 118,000 Indians were working in the United States on temporary visas. That was 44 percent of the total number of people with those visas in the United States. In 2007, 74,000 Indians were in the United States on student visas, the highest number for any country except South Korea

Fighting for Taxi Drivers' Rights

Of course, not every immigrant from South Asia is a successful professional or entrepreneur. South Asian–

As leader of the Taxi Workers Alliance, Bhairavi Desai has campaigned for better working conditions for New York City taxi drivers, about two-thirds of whom are South Asian Americans.

American adults include people in all occupations. Some South Asian immigrants in big cities drive taxis. In New York City, it is estimated that two-thirds of taxi drivers are South Asians, mostly Bangladeshi and Punjabi immigrants. Drivers often work long hours for minimal pay and benefits.

Concerned about that situation, Bhairavi Desai, a college graduate and political organizer, became a leader in the Taxi Workers Alliance (TWA). Desai came to Harrison, New Jersey, with her family from Gujarat, India, when she was a young girl. Her father was a lawyer but wound up running a grocery store. He and his family were targets of racist attacks. In 1998, the TWA led the first of what would be several one-day strikes over working conditions and economic issues. By 2007, the group represented more than seven thousand drivers, and Desai was its executive director.

Customers examine the wares at a New York City street fair, part of a day-long celebration of Pakistani Independence Day.

CHAPTER FOUR

MAKING A NEW LIFE

Immigrants around the world try to adjust to working and carrying on day-to-day life in a new society. Many draw strength for that adjustment from their own traditions and want to preserve them. Still, most immigrants try to **assimilate** (fit in with the new culture) even as they work to preserve their native cultural heritage.

For many immigrants, language, dress, religion, and customs may place them outside the everyday life they see around them. Many South Asian immigrants have the advantage of being able to speak English. But many do not. South Asian immigrants may also have appearances and distinctive dress that identify them as "foreign." For example, most Sikh men wear turbans, and many South Asian

One Person's Story: Balancing Between Cultures

Keva Puri (name changed at her request) was born in the United States in 1973, the youngest of three daughters of Indian immigrants. Her father was a doctor. When she was young, her family moved to Short Hills, New Jersey, "which was very white," Puri says.

She remembers a time as a girl when her school chorus was singing a traditional song of another culture, but not Indian. "Kids were making fun of the song," she remembers. "I was embarrassed. I thought, 'What if they come back to my house and see the Indian decorations there?'"

Puri says she grew up "pretty assimilated," and most of her friends were white. (Her eldest sister "assimilated" in a more radical way. She dyed her naturally dark hair blond, and she cut it in a lopsided style.)

The Puris made frequent trips back to their native village in India. From these trips, Keva learned about her Indian heritage. She also did a school project constructing a family tree that went back five generations. Sometimes her family got together with other Indian families to sing *bhajans*, Hindu devotional songs. Like many younger South Asian Americans, Puri wished she had learned more about Hinduism. But again, as with many immigrants, constraints of time and distance made that difficult. When she married, in 2007, she had a Hindu wedding, but the festivities also included the music of Ireland, her new husband's native land.

Muslim women wear headscarves.

The immigrants' "differences" may cause them to be singled out for discrimination. That's just one reason that many immigrants choose to locate in communities where other immigrants from their country already live.

The area around Devon Avenue, in the northwestern suburbs of Chicago, is a traditional home of Pakistani, Bangladeshi, and Indian communities. Jackson Heights, in the borough of Queens in New York City, has a large and thriving Indian-American community, while thousands of Pakistani Americans live in the Midwood neighborhood in Brooklyn, New York. Among the newer places where "Little Indias" can be found are Cary, North Carolina, and the Hilcroft area in Houston, Texas.

After decades of steady immigration and economic success for many immigrants, many South Asian Americans have moved from cities to the suburbs. Fremont, California, in the San Francisco area, and Artesia, outside Los Angeles, have large South Asian–American populations. Nearly 20,000 Indian Americans live in Edison, New Jersey. Millbourne, Pennsylvania, outside Philadelphia, is the U.S. town with the highest percentage of South Asians. More than 40 percent of its residents are Indian Americans.

Practicing, and Adapting, One's Religion

Raymond Brady Williams, a humanities professor at Wabash College, in Indiana, has written about the Hindu religion and its practice in North America. He describes different ways in which South Asians have found it comfortable to practice their religions outside South Asia, including what he labels individual and ethnic ways of practicing. Having a Hindu marriage ceremony might be considered an individual way of practicing.

A group of immigrants in southern California, all of whom came from the southern Indian state of Kerala, began to meet together in the 1990s. This is an example of the ethnic model for practicing Hinduism. Their activities were described by author Prema Kurien in *Becoming American by Becoming Hindu: Indian Americans Take Their Place at the Multicultural Table*. Getting together informally for Hindu activities is a common practice among immigrants. Hinduism is a complex religion with many varieties. Much of the traditional religious practice takes place in the home, rather than at a central temple. The immigrants who came to southern California from Kerala formed a group called OHM, which stands for Organization of Hindu Malayalees. (People from Kerala who speak the Malayalam language are called Malayalees.) The group meets once a month in members' homes for *pooja* (worship). The group's name, OHM, is a mystical syllable in the Sanskrit language. It is usually chanted at the beginning or end of Hindu prayers or readings.

The OHM poojas begin with chanting (in Sanskrit). The members also sing call-and-response bhajans (devotional songs) and study verses from the Bhagavad Gita, a key Hindu text. A vegetarian South Indian meal concludes the gathering. Besides practicing their religion, the group members raise money for social service organizations, including some that finance projects in India. One teenage boy described the meetings like this: "It made me finally comfortable as an Indian. I realized that there were many other people out there who are like me . . . and that I am not by myself." One of the parents put the value of the poojas this way: "What is the most important thing parents should impart to their children? Values . . . ethical principles of living. If we do this properly, they may have some adjustment difficulties . . . but then they will be set for life."

Pressures in the Family

Immigrant parents and their children don't always share the same views of the immigrant experience. The normal disputes that all parents and children have can be even more complicated when issues of immigrant heritage are mixed in. Young South Asian Americans, who were born in the United States or came to the country when they were very young, face the pressure of living in an American culture of choices and individuality that is very different from their parents' native culture. Sunaina Jain, a psychologist in Georgia, put it this way to John Blake of the *Atlanta Journal-Constitution* for a February 3, 2002, article:

> "They're living in a culture that's so individual, perhaps over-focused on individuality: what I want, what I feel, what my dreams are. South Asian culture is totally not about that. It's about we, the family, fitting in and living up to what's expected rather than having your own voice."

The neighborhood around Devon Avenue in the Chicago area has a large South Asian community.

Another tension, especially in the homes of some newly arrived families, can come from the fact that the children have learned English in school and speak it better than their parents. That can give the children the burden of increased responsibility to help their parents cope with aspects of American life, and it also gives the children power that can lead to resentments between the generations.

The role of women in South Asian-American families can be another difficult issue. Traditionally, the father is the figure of authority in South Asian cultures. But in many Indian-American families, the mother is also likely to be a successful professional. South Asian immigrants often think that American society is too permissive and that young people have too many freedoms. But at the same time, many young South Asian Americans appreciate the choices that are open to women in the United States.

The story of Geeta Mehta illustrates one path of change in the roles of South Asian women. Mehta's mother, Indra Rani, was such a good student in Batala, India, in the 1940s that she earned a scholarship to continue her studies in a college after she finished high school. But Geeta's grandfather asked the school principal not to even tell Indra about the scholarship. She married at the age of twenty. Three decades later, Geeta's parents encouraged her to earn a degree in architecture in New Delhi, and she won an Indian government scholarship to study abroad. She came to the United States and got her master's degree in architecture and urban design at Columbia University, in New York City. She returned to India to work, as required by her scholarship agreement. Mehta later moved back to the United States and got her U.S. citizenship, raised a family, and lived around the world. She became a professor of art history and architecture at Temple University, in Philadelphia, and in 2008 was working at the school's program in Tokyo, Japan.

Questions of dating and marriage can often be a point of crisis for immigrant families. Older South Asian immigrants may have had their marriages arranged by their parents and may not have a good understanding of American-style dating. Like Jewish or Italian or other immigrants before them, South Asian–American parents may want their children to marry South Asians who share their culture and also, importantly, their religion. Many South Asian Americans do marry other South Asians. But, as South Asians become more numerous and more integrated into American society, it can be expected that, like immigrant groups before them, they will be more likely to intermarry with non–South Asians.

School Pressures

South Asian youths also face distinct pressures in school. Some of those pressures were studied in a 2004 report by the Council for Asian American Children and Families (CACF). The report was called "Hidden in Plain View: An Overview of the Needs of Asian American Students in the Public School System."

One pressure comes from belonging to a so-called model minority, a group that is **stereotyped** as being composed of high achievers who thrive without having to struggle to get ahead. It is true that South Asian families generally place a very high priority on education, and many South Asian–American students do well in school. But of course, in any ethnic group, individuals succeed to different degrees and in different ways.

The model-minority prejudice puts extra pressure on students. Sometimes it means that even though South Asians are expected to do well, they may not receive the support in school that they need to achieve that success. One Indian-American high school student told CACF, "We're working hard, and someone assumes that you're just born with it."

Another challenge for students can be a lack of information about South Asians in the school curriculum. "When they teach about Asian culture, they never talk about modern Asia," said one Pakistani-American student about the way she was taught history. "We need to learn about Asian Americans."

Harassment or bullying can be another problem that immigrant students face. "When September 11 happened, people . . . labeled you a Muslim, calling you a terrorist because you're South Asian," said a girl who attended high school in Queens, New York.

Life in Little Pakistan, New York

Midwood is a middle-class and working-class neighborhood in Brooklyn, New York. Coney Island Avenue is one of the neighborhood's "Main Streets." Food markets, video outlets, fabric stores, travel shops, health clinics, restaurants, and places to transfer money abroad line the avenue. Signs advertise in English, Spanish, Russian, Hebrew, and also in Urdu. Urdu is the native language of Midwood's thousands of Pakistani immigrants, who give the neighborhood its nickname, "Little Pakistan."

Food markets and restaurants offer *halal* food, which meets the dietary laws of the Islamic religion. A few Muslim women wear *burkahs*, outer cloaks that totally cover their bodies, except for their eyes (though blue jeans

Nupur Lala shows her joy after winning the 1999 Scripps Howard National Spelling Bee.

Spelling S-u-c-c-e-s-s

People who use big words but don't really say anything can be described as having *logorrhea*, excessive talkiness. In 1999, fourteen-year-old Nupur Lala spelled logorrhea correctly to win the annual Scripps Howard National Spelling Bee in Washington, D.C. Lala's victory began a streak for Indian-American students, who won the contest half a dozen more times in the early 2000s.

In an interview with ESPN, Lala pointed to the importance of education in Indian-American homes as a reason for Indian Americans' success in spelling bees. "Indian parents see this as a prime opportunity for their children to learn the benefits of competition in an arena where it's not necessarily the fastest or biggest kid who will be the winner. And where nothing but sheer hard work will bring you success," Lala said.

Lala not only won the competition but ended up being the star of a popular documentary movie about the 1999 competition, *Spellbound*.

The Midwood section of Brooklyn, New York, is a diverse neighborhood including many Pakistani Americans.

might show down by the women's shoes). Other women wear green, orange, or purple headscarves or *salwars*—long flowing tops that are worn over pajama-like pants. Some Pakistani men wear long *kurta* shirts. More men than women favor Western dress.

The Council of Peoples Organization (COPO) is a community center on Coney Island Avenue in Midwood. It serves South Asians, offering free English and computer classes and providing legal assistance. COPO estimates that the average household income among South Asians in Brooklyn is only about $12,000 a year for families of four to six people. Common jobs for the men are taxi driver, restaurant worker, store clerk, and laborer. Most women don't work.

Post 9/11 Problems

COPO was founded in February 2002 by Mohammad (Moe) Razvi to help the community in the aftermath of the terrorist attacks of September 11, 2001. Razvi came to the United States from Pakistan as a young boy. He grew up in public housing projects in Brooklyn.

To counter post-9/11 anti-Muslim and anti-Pakistani sentiment, this Pakistani-American store owner in Chicago displayed a sign opposing terrorism.

The September 11 attacks spelled trouble for the Pakistani community. After the attacks, some five hundred people in the neighborhood, almost all men, were picked up by the authorities for questioning. No information was immediately available about the men, Razvi said. (Some were later deported for immigration law violations.) In 2002, Pakistani men in the United States with valid visas were required to register with the federal government under a special registration program. South Asians also became the victims of hate crimes committed by people who associated them with the terrorist attacks.

COPO worked with the FBI and other federal and local authorities to protect the rights of community members. It advocated on behalf of the community to U.S. Citizenship and Immigration Services, urging the agency to clear up the backlog of background checks for immigrants waiting to become naturalized citizens. Despite COPO's efforts, Razvi estimated that 20,000 Pakistanis decided to leave Brooklyn and the United States after the special registration program went into effect in 2002.

These people have chosen a
peaceful beachfront location
for their yoga exercises.

CHAPTER FIVE

CHANGING THE AMERICAN CULTURE

C utting-edge Internet and environmental technologies; ancient medical wisdom; ideas about Islam in the modern world; yoga; **bhangra music**; curry— these represent just a few of the many ways in which South Asian Americans and their heritage are enriching life in the United States.

Alternative Medicine

The surge of South Asians who came to the United States beginning in the late 1960s included thousands of doctors who helped fill a growing need for physicians around the country. More recently, some South Asians have been in the forefront of the movement toward alternative and

Dr. Deepak Chopra at the Chopra
Center and Spa in New York City.

preventive health care. Many of their approaches draw
on traditional Asian practices. According to a 2004 U.S.
government study, 36 percent of American adults used
some form of alternative medicine.

Born in New Delhi, Deepak Chopra came to the United
States in 1970. He worked as a doctor in hospitals in
New Jersey and Massachusetts. In 1996, he founded the
Chopra Center for Wellbeing, in Carlsbad, California. (A
second center, in New York City, opened in 2004.) Chopra's
philosophy blends Western technological medicine and
thousands of years of traditional Asian medical practice.
Through yoga, meditation, and other means rooted in the
ancient teachings of Hinduism, Chopra encourages people
to find "the seduction of silence." He says that this peaceful

state can produce "creative inspiration, knowledge, and stability."

Chopra is a proponent of *Ayurveda*, which means the "science of life" in the ancient Indian language of Sanskrit. Through Ayurveda, people seek to balance what practitioners see as the three basic natural forces and energies (earth, wind, and fire) that govern health and well-being. Diet, herbs, aromas, massage, music, and meditation are used to achieve that balance.

The practice of yoga is probably the most popular approach to well-being that has made its way from South Asia to the United States. A Sanskrit word for "union," yoga can be thought of as a set of practices and beliefs to help a person be healthy and energetic. The history of yoga goes back to Hindu practitioners more than 2,500 years ago. When most people in the United States talk about yoga today, they are talking about a series of *asanas*. These are disciplined body poses that promote strength, flexibility, and energy. A Harris Interactive poll in 2008 for *Yoga Journal* found that 15.8 million Americans had practiced yoga in the previous year. About three-quarters of them were women.

Islam in the Modern World

Pakistani American Fazlur Rahman (1919–1988) was a prominent Islamic scholar and contributor to the ongoing intellectual discussion of interpretations of Islam in the modern world. He taught for nearly thirty years at the University of Chicago and served as an adviser to the U.S. State Department. Rahman was born in 1919, in what is today the North-West Frontier Province of Pakistan. He came to the United States in the 1960s after leaving a position in the Pakistani government, where he worked to further integrate Islam into the everyday life of the country.

Rahman is considered an Islamic modernist. He called for a rejuvenation of Islamic educational and intellectual life. He advocated a moderate position between, on the one hand, secularists who argue for abandoning Islam as a way to help Muslim societies advance and, on the other, strict interpreters of the Koran, Islam's holy book. Rahman

YouTube co-founder Jawed Karim (*right*) chats with the chancellor of the University of Illinois before delivering a speech at the 2007 graduation ceremonies.

argued that interpretations of the Koran needed to show some flexibility to fit into a modern world. He argued that much of the Koran was revealed "in, although not merely for, a given historical context" and, therefore, that some portions might not be applicable to modern life.

Advancing Technology

When many people think of South Asian Americans, they think of technology. Among the leading technologists and businesspeople in the United States is Vinod Khosla. Khosla was born in Pune, India. He came to the United States in the 1970s to study after his soymilk business venture in India failed. In 1982, he founded Sun Microsystems, whose computers, programs, and processes played critical roles in the Internet revolution.

In the early twenty-first century, Khosla continued to be involved in software development, including popular applications for Facebook. But he was also a venture capitalist, someone who helps new companies get the money they need to grow and develop. One of Khosla's focuses was on "green" environmental technologies to help reduce pollution and fight global warming. Companies he became involved with were working to reduce industrial carbon emissions, to convert biomass (organic waste products such as wood, cotton, and unused portions of agricultural crops) to fuel, and to create more efficient combustion engines (the type of engine used to power most automobiles).

A much younger techno star with South Asian roots is Jawed Karim, co-founder of YouTube, the video-sharing

Internet site. Karim was born in Germany in 1979 and grew up there with his Bangladeshi father and his German mother, both scientists. He came to the United States in 1992. He met YouTube co-founders Chad Hurley and Steve Chen while working at PayPal, the online payment company. They worked together on YouTube before Karim left to pursue graduate studies at Stanford University.

Two events in 2004, the highly destructive Asian tsunami and Janet Jackson's "wardrobe malfunction" at the Super Bowl halftime show, gave the young men the idea for a video-sharing site, which developed into YouTube. In a graduation address at the University of Illinois in 2007, Karim said that the main idea of the site was that "anyone who has a good idea can take that idea and make it happen." Karim told of how he first failed to get into the school's computer science program. But he followed up with the admissions department and won admission. "Persistence pays off," he told the graduates.

Bhangra Music

Waving hands, bending knees, and bouncing feet—that's bhangra dancing. Bhangra music and dance have their roots in the harvest ceremonies of the Punjab. Today, the wailing melodies and insistent drumming of bhangra music are growing in popularity in the United States and around the world. Rekha Malhotra, better known as DJ Rekha, champions bhangra music, and international music star Wyclef Jean appeared on her first album. (Though Rekha's parents wanted her to be a doctor or a lawyer, they were proud when

DJ Rekha at work creating a mixture of Punjabi bhangra, dance hall, and hip hop beats.

her first CD came out in 2007.)

DJ Rekha ("first name DJ, last name Rekha") spins mixes of bhangra, dance hall, and hip-hop beats. She says that those rhythms reflect the mixed South-Asian, African-American, and Caribbean-American communities where she grew up in suburban New York. She's proud that the "basement bhangra" parties that she has hosted around the United States have drawn people of diverse cultures.

South Asian Cooking

In Great Britain, where more than 2 percent of the population is South Asian, Indian food is so popular that people joke that chicken *tikka masala* is the European country's national dish. South Asian cooking, or cuisine, is also

Tandoori chicken gets its color from the seasonings
used to flavor it and gets its name from the clay
pot, or tandoor, in which it is cooked.

popular in the United States. In 2008, one website listed more than 250 Indian restaurants in California alone.

South Asian cuisine is as varied as South Asians themselves. Rice, legumes (such as lentils and chick peas), and vegetables are the centerpiece of much South Asian cuisine. *Dal bhat* (rice with lentils) is a staple dish of the Nepalese. Most Nepalese dishes are vegetarian. *Thalis*, or meals, in the Gujarat region of India also tend to be vegetarian. *Tandoori* dishes, popular in the Punjab and elsewhere, get their name from the clay *tandoor* pot that the food is cooked in. In dishes like tandoori chicken, the meat is marinated in yogurt before cooking. The yellow or red color comes from annatto seeds or saffron. Fish tandoori and shrimp tandoori are also popular, but because Islam forbids the consumption of pork, pork tandoori won't be found on most South Asian menus.

Of course, when people think of South Asian food, they think of curry. But curry dishes from South Asia don't just mean something with curry powder from the supermarket. In most South Asian cooking, curries are based on a mix of spices known as *garam masala*. Many South Asian families have their own recipes, but the spices for garam masala might include chilies, cinnamon, cardamom, cumin, coriander, bay leaves, and pepper cloves. Traditionally, the spices are ground together with a mortar and pestle. The spice mix is often used to flavor stews of meats or vegetables.

Chai tea—a traditional Indian preparation that includes boiled milk along with the tea—is now widely available and popular in the United States.

Louisiana governor Bobby Jindal, the first Indian American to hold the governorship of a U.S. state, greets schoolchildren during an early 2009 public appearance.

CHAPTER SIX

LOOKING TO THE FUTURE

At the August 2008 Democratic National Convention in Denver, Colorado, the Indian American Leadership Initiative held a reception. This event was believed to be the first South Asian–American political meeting at a major party convention. As the number of South Asian Americans continues to climb, many people expect that the political influence of South Asian Americans will also continue to grow. In fact, that is already happening.

Indian Americans in Politics

Louisiana is a southern state proud of its football, its food, and its claim as the birthplace of jazz music. In 2007, Louisiana gained a new distinction by electing the first Indian-American governor in the United States, thirty-six-year-old Bobby Jindal.

Students Advocating for the Future

Future South Asian American leaders are being trained today, even in high schools. The Coalition for Asian Children and Families is the only pan-Asian children's advocacy program in the United States. (Pan-Asian means that the group tries to speak for all Asian immigrants—including East Asians, Southeast Asians, and Pacific Islanders, as well as South Asians.) One goal of CACF is to train student leaders in its Asian-American Student Advocacy Project (ASAP), led by Wendy Cheung.

The high school students in ASAP get training in public speaking, in advocacy, and in their Asian-American heritage. They identify issues that are important to their communities—for instance, programs for students who are English language learners—and then try to get changes made that will advance those issues. One recent success achieved by the young leaders was winning greater awareness of Asian-American history month (which is May) at some of their schools.

ASAP leaders also advocated for more mental health resources in schools. Their goal was to better support students who were being harassed and to reduce harassment. In that effort, however, "the students learned one of the hard lessons" that comes with leadership, said Vanessa Leung, CACF deputy director. School budget cuts meant that additional school mental health programs could not be funded.

Jindal was born in Baton Rouge, Louisiana, in 1971, six months after his mother came to the United States to study nuclear physics. His family was from the Punjab. After attending Brown University and winning a prestigious Rhodes scholarship to study in England, Jindal worked in government in the education and health care fields. He was elected to Congress as a Republican in 2004.

Jindal won election as governor in a state where Indian Americans make up less than one percent of the population. His success can be explained in part by his conservative politics and by his reputation for honesty and efficiency as a government administrator. But Jindal was also successful at portraying himself as a regular Louisianan. In college, he converted from Hinduism to Roman Catholicism. As a boy, he didn't want to be called by his given name, Piyush. He wanted to be called "Bobby," after the character in the TV show *The Brady Bunch*.

By 2009, several other South Asian Americans had been elected to seats in state legislatures.

Continuing Change

The growing South Asian-American population is expected to have a growing influence throughout American society, not just in politics. Like many Muslims, Moe Razvi of COPO believes that a growing South Asian Muslim population in the United States can help spread a "moderate" Islam that places an emphasis on the rights of the individual and the rights of women.

Indian-American actor Kal Penn in a 2008 episode of the TV series *House*. (He left the show in 2009.)

As more South Asian Americans become prominent in the media, portrayals of South Asians are likely to become more rounded than such stereotypical characters as Apu Nahasapeemapetilon on the television show *The Simpsons*. That evolution will likely bring more portrayals like the character of Gogol Ganguli in the movie *The Namesake*.

A Family Giving Back

As South Asian immigrants succeed in the United States, more and more are getting involved in projects to support their homeland. Krishen Mehta came to Denver, Colorado, from Delhi, India, in 1969 to study business. Like the Punjabi immigrants of seventy years earlier, Mehta was able to make the journey with the help of his family, who had mortgaged their house to help fund his trip.

India at that time restricted the amount of money that could be taken out of the country. Once Mehta arrived in the United States, he wasn't able to get more funds from his family. That put a lot of pressure on him. "We couldn't fail. What would our families think?" But Mehta worked hard and benefited from what he called a "welcoming" environment in the United States. "We came from a society where the struggle for survival was so intense. Now we were in a receptive environment where the same initiative produced multiple times what could be done in India," Mehta explained.

Mehta became a U.S. citizen, in part to ease the process of having his Indian wife, Geeta, an architect, join him. He eventually became a partner in the PriceWaterhouseCoopers accounting firm and, with his wife, raised a family. One of his adult sons returned to India in 2008, in part to "give back" to the family's homeland but also to pursue the opportunities now available in India. Krishen and Geeta Mehta founded Asia Initiatives (AI) in 2000. AI provides "microcredit" loans (small loans given to people who probably would not qualify for a traditional business loan but who have a good idea for a business) to people, mostly women, and to small businesses in Asia. The Mehtas say that AI is another way of giving back, not just to the Mehtas' Indian homeland but to people throughout South Asia.

Geeta and Krishen Mehta (*center*) visiting one of the projects they helped fund in India.

Played by Indian American Kal Penn (born Kalpen Suresh Modi), the teenaged Indian American Gogol learns the power of his Indian roots. (Penn took a break from his acting career in 2009 to join the White House Office of Public Liaison. In that new role, his focus, in part, was on communication between the White House and Asian-American communities.)

South Asians will certainly continue to be influential in the U.S. economy. YouTube founder Jawed Karim, for example, went on to create Youniversity Ventures, a company that helps young entrepreneurs launch their businesses.

A South Asian Safety Net

The number of South Asians arriving in the United States continues to grow. But the rapid economic growth in India is offering South Asians more opportunities to pursue their dreams without leaving home and provides a strong lure for South Asian Americans thinking of returning home. One software developer told the *Boston Globe* in 2005 that he had turned down a permanent job in Boston, preferring to return to India.

Shoba Narayan is an Indian writer who spent many years in the United States but now lives in Bangalore, India. She has written that the generation of Indians graduating from college at the end of the first decade of the twenty-first century "view India as a safety net that they can always fall back on, instead of something they want to escape from." Echoing the dreams of the first South Asian immigrants a hundred years earlier, Narayan says, "Unlike my generation, this one can go back home again."

FACTS ABOUT INDIAN AMERICANS

Characteristic	Indian Americans	Percentage for Indian Americans	Total U.S. Population	Percentage for U.S. Population
Total population	2,482,141		299,398,485	
Male	1,315,535	53%	146,705,258	49%
Female	1,166,606	47%	152,693,227	51%
Median age (years)	32		36	
Under 5 years old	198,571	8%	20,957,894	7%
18 years and over	1,886,427	76%	224,548,864	75%
65 years and over	148,928	6%	35,927,818	12%
Average family size	3		3	
Number of households	815,231		111,617,402	
Owner-occupied housing units	448,377	55%	74,783,659	67%
Renter-occupied housing units	366,854	45%	36,833,743	33%
People age 25 and over with high school diploma or higher	1,503,433	90%	164,729,046	84%
People age 25 and over with bachelor's degree or higher	1,152,632	69%	52,948,622	27%
Foreign born	1,840,139	74%	37,547,789	13%
Number of people who speak a language other than English at home (population 5 years and older)	1,811,698	80%	55,807,878	20%
Median family income	$87,484		$58,526	
Per capita income	$34,895		$25,267	
Individuals living below the poverty level	198,571	8%	38,921,803	13%

Source: U.S. Bureau of the Census, 2006 American Community Survey estimates

FACTS ABOUT PAKISTANI AMERICANS

Characteristic	Pakistani Americans	Percentage for Pakistani Americans	Total U.S. Population	Percentage for U.S. Population
Total population	194,462		299,398,485	
Male	106,954	55%	146,705,258	49%
Female	87,508	45%	152,693,227	51%
Median age (years)	29		36	
Under 5 years old	17,502	9%	20,957,894	7%
18 years and over	134,179	69%	224,548,864	75%
65 years and over	7,778	4%	35,927,818	12%
Average family size	4		3	
Number of households	51,303		111,617,402	
Owner-occupied housing units	25,652	50%	74,783,659	67%
Renter-occupied housing units	25,652	50%	36,833,743	33%
People age 25 and over with high school diploma or higher	96,095	87%	164,729,046	84%
People age 25 and over with bachelor's degree or higher	59,645	54%	52,948,622	27%
Foreign born	137,702	71%	37,547,789	13%
Number of people who speak a language other than English at home (population 5 years and older)	153,195	87%	55,807,878	20%
Median family income	$59,306		$58,526	
Per capita income	$23,024		$25,267	
Individuals living below the poverty level	33,059	17%	38,921,803	13%

Source: U.S. Bureau of the Census, 2006 American Community Survey estimates

GLOSSARY

assimilate: How people who have moved to another country adopt the customs and behaviors of the people in their new environment.

bhangra music: A traditional folk music from South Asia's Punjab region that is now popular internationally.

discrimination: Unfair treatment of a person or group based on such characteristics as race, ethnic group, or religion.

entrepreneur: Someone who starts, supplies the money for, and operates a new business.

expatriate: A person from one country who chooses to, or sometimes is forced to, leave his or her native country and live in a different country.

gateway city: A city that attracts new immigrants, often because earlier immigrants from the same country already live there.

Hinduism: One of the world's largest religions and the principal religion of India. Hinduism is built around the principle of Brahman, the divine interconnectedness of everything. Hinduism's many gods are aspects of the divine. To escape the meaningless cycle of death and rebirth, Hindus seek to improve their karma through good deeds.

Islam: One of the world's largest religions and the principal religion of Pakistan. Followers of Islam, called Muslims, believe in one god, Allah, whose message was revealed to the prophet Muhammad in the early seventh century C.E. The five "pillars of Islam" are acknowledging Allah, praying daily, giving to charity, fasting during the month of Ramadan, and making a pilgrimage to the holy city of Mecca.

Muslim: A follower of the religion of Islam.

naturalization: The process by which people not born citizens of a country can become its citizens.

nonimmigrant visa: An official approval to enter a country for a limited amount of time but not to reside there permanently. Student visas, work visas, and tourist visas are examples of nonimmigrant visas.

permanent resident status: The status held by immigrants to the United States who have been approved by the government to live and work permanently there. Permanent residents can generally apply to become citizens after five years.

precedent: A court decision that is later used as a guide for deciding other similar cases.

Punjab: A fertile region of South Asia lying in what is now northwestern India and eastern Pakistan.

Sanskrit: An ancient language of India. Important Hindu texts are written in Sanskrit, which is no longer commonly spoken.

Sikhism: A religion founded in the sixteenth century C.E. that is followed by many people in the Punjab region. Sikhs believe in a cycle of reincarnation that, if one lives an exemplary life, can result in merging with God.

stereotype: To have an oversimplified, and overly general, characterization of a person or group or people.

temporary resident: A person who has come to the United States for a limited time period, perhaps to study, and who does not plan to stay in the country permanently.

temporary work visa: A U.S. government document that grants permission for a person to come to the United States to work for a fixed period of time.

visa: A document allowing entry into a country.

TO FIND OUT MORE

Further Reading

Helweg, Arthur W. *Strangers in a Not-So-Strange Land: Indian American Immigrants in the Global Age.* Belmont, CA: Wadsworth/Thomson, 2004.

Ingram, Scott. *South Asian Americans.* Milwaukee, WI: World Almanac Library, 2007.

Luce, Edward. *In Spite of the Gods: The Rise of Modern India.* New York: Doubleday, 2007.

Rangaswamy, Padma. *Indian Americans.* New York: Chelsea House, 2007.

Sheehan, Sean, and Shahrezad Samiuddin. *Pakistan.* New York: Marshall Cavendish Benchmark, 2005.

Srinivasan, Radhika, and Leslie Jermyn. *India.* New York: Marshall Cavendish Benchmark, 2002.

Tharoor, Shashi. *The Elephant, the Tiger, and the Cell Phone: Reflections on India, the Emerging 21st-Century Power.* New York: Arcade Publishing, 2007.

Websites

http://www.lib.berkeley.edu/SSEAL/echoes.html
This site hosts an exhibit by the University of California at Berkeley Library entitled "Echoes of Freedom: South Asian Pioneers in California, 1899–1965." It includes images of early South Asian immigrants to the United States.

http://www.littleindia.com
This site offers news of India and Indian life overseas.

http://www.pbs.org/rootsinthesand
This site, which complements the *Roots in the Sand* television program, explores the history of early-twentieth-century Punjabi immigrants to California and the families and communities that arose out of marriages with Mexican-American women.

BIBLIOGRAPHY

The author found these sources especially helpful when researching this volume:

Investing in America: The Indian Story. New York: U.S.-India Business Council, 2008.

Kalita, S. Mitra. *Suburban Sahibs: Three Immigrant Families and Their Passage from India to America*. New Brunswick, NJ: Rutgers University Press, 2003.

Kamdar, Mira. *Motiba's Tattoos: A Granddaughter's Journey from America into Her Indian Family's Past*. New York: Plume, 2001.

Khandelwal, Madhulika S. *Becoming American, Being Indian: An Immigrant Community in New York City*. Ithaca, NY: Cornell University Press, 2002.

Mohammad-Arif, Aminah. *Salaam America: South Asian Muslims in New York*. Translated by Sarah Patey. London: Anthem Press, 2002.

Naryan, Shoba. "The 'India Option.'" *Little India*, September 9, 2008. Published at http://www.littleindia.com/news/127/ARTICLE/3701/2008-09-09.html

The author conducted personal interviews with the following people quoted in this book, and the author and the publisher wish to thank them for their cooperation:

Daughter of Dr. Amin (name changed to protect privacy)
Keva Puri (name changed at her request)
Vikram and Rekha Ganvir (names changed at their request)
Wendy Cheung   Vanessa Leung
Geeta and Krishen Mehta   Mohammad Razvi

Notes:

Chapter 2:

Page 23: "Walk and bend, bend and walk." Takaki, Ronald. "East Indian Immigrants Face Discrimination in America." *In* Ruggiero, Adriane, ed. *The East Indians*. Detroit: Greenhaven Press/Thomson Gale, 2006.

Chapter 4:

Page 48: "It made me finally comfortable . . ." and "What is the most important thing parents . . ." Kurien, Prema. "Becoming American by Becoming Hindu: Indian Americans Take Their Place at the Multicultural Table." *In* Warner, R. Stephen, and Judith G. Wittner, eds. *Gatherings in Diaspora: Religious Communities and the New Immigration*. Philadelphia: Temple University Press, 1998.

Chapter 6:

Page 71: ". . . view India as a safety net. . . ." Naryan, Shoba. "The 'India Option.'" *Little India*, September 9, 2008. http://www.littleindia.com/news/127/ARTICLE/3701/2008-09-09.html

All websites were accessible as of April 4, 2009.

INDEX

Page numbers in **boldface** are illustrations, tables, and charts.

About the Series Consultant

Judith Ann Warner is a Professor of Sociology and Criminal Justice at Texas A&M International University (TAMIU), located in Laredo, Texas, near the U.S.-Mexico border. She has specialized in the study of race and ethnic relations, focusing on new immigrants to the United States and their social incorporation into American society. Professor Warner is the editor of and contributed a number of essays to *Battleground Immigration* (2009), a collection of essays on immigration and related national security issues. Recognition of her work includes the 2007 Distance Educator of the Year Award and the 1991 Scholar of the Year Award at TAMIU.

About the Author

Ken Park has worked in educational and reference publishing for more than twenty-five years. He published seven editions of *The World Almanac and Book of Facts*, including five #1 *New York Times* bestsellers. He also published *The World Almanac for Kids* and *Yo! I Know: Brain Building Quizzes*. Online, Park produced the award-winning Reference Suite @ Facts.com and the Facts*for*Learning reference site. He lives with his wife and daughter in Brooklyn, New York. This is his first book for Marshall Cavendish Benchmark.